YEAR OF THE
Barn Owl

Devised and illustrated by
Terry Riley
Written by John Andrews

J M Dent & Sons Ltd
London Toronto Melbourne

It was night and the countryside was almost silent. Overhead, a warm bright moon shone in the cloudless, late-summer sky. Deep, dark shadows lay along hedges and under the trees. There, shrews scurried, searching for beetles and slugs. Long-tailed mice feasted on the ripe nuts newly fallen to the woodland floor. Amongst the grass roots, voles trotted purposefully along their covered runs. A dormouse clambered carefully amongst the twining honeysuckle high above the ground and disturbed a roosting wren which churred briefly in irritation. Then silence again fell over the wood and the fields. Like the wren, almost all birds were asleep. Only one was awake and she was busy about her own hunting.

Round the corner of the wood she flew slowly, on long pale wings, drifting close to the ground, peering with huge eyes into every tussock and bush. She made no sound at all as she passed close by.

A few weeks ago, the owl had been a downy chick, sharing a nest in a hollow tree with her eight brothers and sisters. Each night, her parents had brought many small animals to feed their ever-hungry brood. But when the youngsters had left their nest, they had to begin to look after themselves. Life suddenly became much harder. The young birds had to learn how to catch their own food.

This female had wandered far, alone and often hungry, before she found the warm valley woods and fields where food was plentiful. For the last week, she had hunted here, growing plump and strong.

After a month, the young barn owl grew familiar with her new home. She soon found a place to roost during the daytime. High up inside the roof of an old barn, she sat in the shadows drowsing and blinking, listening to the chirrup of sparrows outside and the skittering of their small feet as they hopped on the sunlit tiles.

As dusk fell, the sparrows prepared to go to roost. Then the owl awoke, hungry and ready to hunt. First she stretched each wing in turn, spreading the long, soft flight feathers like fingers. Then she ruffled up her body feathers and gave herself a good shake. Finally she let them settle back into the smooth, creamy brown coat that protected her against wind and rain.

Tonight she would need such protection. As she swooped out through the open barn door, the first gusts of a rising wind buffeted her. At first she rode on it, letting herself be blown along but, once she decided to start hunting, she had to turn and flap hard against it. The wind shook the bushes and the grass, making so many movements and rustles that she was confused. The small animals moved safely, unheard and unseen by the pale bird.

At last she came to the beginning of the wood. Overhead, branches rattled together and the autumn leaves blew away, swirling in clouds. But near the ground it was sheltered and calm. Here the owl perched, alert, and soon she caught her supper.

After the autumn gales, winter came. Prey became much more difficult to catch. The shrews were hunting their food down under the deepest drifts of fallen leaves. The voles were safe in their runways beneath the snow, eating their stores of grass stems. The dormice were securely in bed, sleeping until the spring.

The owl hunted through the long nights and into the cold light of dawn. Often she returned hungry to roost and slowly she grew thinner. Each day, she carefully preened her feathers so that, when she fluffed them all out, they made a warm coat against the icy air. Before it grew dark, she set out to hunt again.

Flying low, she passed slowly across the fields. The evening sky held the threat of more snow. She was beginning to grow weak. If she did not find food soon, she would die.

Quite by chance, her luck changed. She flew low over the top of an old stone wall, and heard at once the rustle of small birds shifting nervously in a sheltered bush. A moment's pause and her long leg reached out to pluck a sleepy finch from its roosting perch.

Gradually, winter turned to spring. The weather grew warmer and the first new green leaves began to sprout. One mild, cloudy night, as the owl sat on a gatepost attentively listening for mice, she saw another barn owl approaching. She flew up at once. He swerved in sudden alarm and she chased him way.

The next night he came back again and weird, shrieking calls rang through the listening woods. He flew round the female, clapping his wings. Pleased by his display, she accepted his company and after a few nights, the two birds flew side by side, talking to each other with strange clicking and growling noises.

During the day they began to share the same roosting place. Here the male would display to her, cheeping and snapping his beak; then stretching up and blowing out his feathers to make himself look as large and impressive as possible. After that, he would sway his head round and round and sidle up close until he could rub his face against hers.

With the better weather, the hunting had become easier and the owls were fit and strong. The female could now develop eggs inside her body. At the same time, she became really used to having the other owl close to her and, at last, the two birds mated. Now there would be chicks in her eggs and she was nearly ready to lay them.

The two birds had already chosen where they would nest. They had found a ledge high up inside an abandoned building. They entered into it through a hole in the roof, made when a gale had torn away several of the heavy tiles. There was also a gap in one wall, like a window, but with no glass in it. Once inside the building, they were in a big dark space, dusty and quiet. There was an old swallow's nest on one roof beam. Stones had fallen from the top of a wall to leave a deep ledge. Generations of jackdaws had piled it with twigs. It was an ideal place for the owls to nest – sheltered and well hidden from the curious eyes of any enemy.

Soon the female laid her first egg. It was round and glossy white and it seemed to shine in the gloom. Two days later, she laid another and from then on, she left the nest only rarely. Most of the time, she sat on the eggs, warming them against her body. She laid two more eggs, making four in all. An older female might have laid several more but, of course, this was her first clutch.

She did not dare leave the eggs for long in case they grew cold and the chicks developing inside them died. Sometimes the male bird brought her food, carrying it hanging from his beak. She would swallow it whole and, twice a day, she coughed up a dry, shiny looking pellet of the bones and fur. The space around the nest became covered with them.

The first chick hatched in early May, a downy little creature that seemed all eyes and feet. At first it could hardly lift its head but it did not take long before it was standing up strongly, eager to be fed.

One at a time over the next ten days, the other three eggs hatched in turn. With each new mouth to feed, the two parent owls were forced to work harder. Throughout the night, they would come and go, carrying mice and voles at first but, as the young birds grew, bringing larger prey.

By now, the older chicks had grown buff-coloured woolly coats, and only the baby was still in white down. Because it was the smallest, the other chicks pushed it aside and made sure they were fed first. Fortunately, there was plenty for everyone and sometimes the largest chick had so much to eat that he sat with the tail of his last meal dangling from his mouth, unable to swallow it.

One night, while both their parents were away hunting, there came a strange scrabbling of claws from below the nest. The young owls had been sleeping in a drowsy, downy heap, but at once their heads shot up. The scrabbling grew louder and a big brown rat with long yellow teeth clambered up on to the nest. The young owls stood up. Spreading their wings and swaying their heads from side to side, trying to look as big and fierce as possible, they hissed loudly through open beaks. The rat could have killed them easily, but it was afraid. It squealed and fled back into the darkness.

Capturing enough food for their large chicks was hard work for the parent owls. The summer nights were short, so as soon as dusk began the adults would set out, flying slowly over the fields and round the woods, stopping to hover at likely places and always looking keenly downwards. Their soft broad wings made no warning sound of their approach.

Both birds made good use of the faint light with their huge, round eyes. But owls' eyes are so big that they cannot swivel them like most creatures. Because of this, they have very flexible necks and turn their heads to look to the side and behind them. In really dark places, they use their ears – large openings hidden under their white feathers – to find their prey.

One very cloudy summer's night, the female sat on the lowest branch of a leafy tree on the edge of a wood. No light reached the ground beneath. She was listening intently. She used her ears like eyes, turning her head towards each faint sound and, just as surely as if she were using her eyes, she knew what had made each noise. A leaf rustled in the breeze. A beetle turned a twig. Then, some small animal scurried briefly. Her head turned towards the sound. It came again and silently she left her perch, gliding down head first towards the spot. At the last moment, she swung her taloned feet forward, reaching out confidently to grasp the invisible prey still hidden in the dark. Then she flew quickly back to the nest to feed an eager chick and return once more to hunting.

All the chicks grew well and by July their woolly coats had been replaced by proper feathers. They spent a lot of time preening to rid themselves of their baby fluff and to keep their new plumage clean and neat. That was not easy in the crowded nest.

To exercise, they flapped as best they could and pushed each other about rather roughly. Eventually, the largest chick launched itself up to the roof hole and peered into the world outside. The darkness seemed to be full of strange shapes and sounds. He was quite pleased to tumble back into his familiar nest when the male owl arrived.

Gradually, over the next few nights, all of the youngsters worked up the courage to look out of the hole. Some of them stayed there for quite a while, getting first choice of the meals their parents brought back. Then one night, three of them left the nest and their parents fed them out on the tiles of the roof. At dawn, they all went back into the safety of the barn.

The smallest owl was still sitting inside. It had been given hardly any food all night and it was feeling very hungry. It was awake and bad-tempered during the day while the other youngsters dozed comfortably. When dusk came again, all four of them left the nest and the youngest bird managed to catch up on its missed meals. Soon their parents would stop feeding them, so the young owls now had to learn to look after themselves.

Born with the natural instinct of hunters, the youngsters began trying to catch things as soon as they left the nest. At first, they could not fly very well but they quickly learned. It was high summer now and the leaves of the trees had lost their spring brightness and were turning to a dull green in the heat. The long spell of fine weather had made it easy for all the birds, the small mammals and other creatures to produce plenty of their own offspring. The fields and hedges were full of things for the young owls to catch.

First they practised pouncing from perches. After that they tried hovering as they peered eagerly into the dried undergrowth. Often they caught nothing but they had left the nest plump and healthy so, though they went hungry, they were not yet in danger of starving.

The young birds gradually moved apart, seeing each other less often. One found rich pickings by an old pond where frogs hopped at night on the banks and were easy to capture. Another – a young male – tried hunting in a wood and was chased off by a big brown owl that would have killed him if it could have caught him. The other two drifted in different directions on their beautiful pale golden wings. Gradually, they learned how to hunt well.

If the weather had been bad, it might have been a different story. When food is scarce and hunting is difficult, young owls can starve and die. As it was, their worst problem came from other birds.

As dawn approached, each youngster would try to find a quiet, shady place to roost. One would press close to the trunk of a tree, another hide in a clump of ivy. But often the keen eyes of some passing bird – perhaps a robin or a tit – would spot one of them and it would give the alarm. Many small birds have a special call that they make when they find a roosting owl. Other birds recognize the sound. They gather round, safely out of reach of the owl's long legs and sharp talons. Whistling and calling, they mob it.

A roosting owl is a danger to all the small birds in the area. By mobbing it, they might drive it away altogether. If not, at least they would all remember where it was sitting, so that later none of them would accidentally get too close and be killed.

Old, wise owls just blink their eyes and wait for the trouble to go away. Youngsters panic, flap about and only attract more trouble. Eventually, all of them learn to ignore these small pests.

Both adults had lost weight while rearing their family but they would soon put it back again. Their plumage had become worn too, with feathers frayed or broken. This was the time of year when they replaced them. A few old feathers moulted out each day, new ones coming in their places and quickly growing to fill the gaps.

The owls spent a lot of time fussing with their feathers. Running their beaks along each one they cleaned and stroked it skilfully into shape. Then they would carefully scratch their head feathers with long claws. Better still, both birds would sit side by side, taking turns to preen each other's face and head.

At dusk, they flew off separately to hunt. One hot, late summer evening, when the sky was still light with afterglow, the female was flying lazily along a line of dusty trees. At the end of it, a man with a shotgun leaned against the trunk of the last tree, looking out over the fields. Not seeing him, the owl drew silently closer.

Suddenly, the white bird appeared almost beside him. He jumped with surprise. She too was startled; she banked and flapped hard to turn away. At the same time, his gun came up. Taking rapid aim, he pulled the trigger. A single pellet cut through her wing tip. As she vanished into the dark, a solitary pale gold feather floated to the ground.

Autumn came. One of the four young owls had died but the other three had found places of their own where they could live. They had become capable hunters and, with luck, would survive the winter.

Bats flickered through the cool evening air, busily catching insects to make them fat before their long winter sleep. Hedgehogs too were preparing for hibernation. Usually, they shuffled along, poking and prying for slugs and beetles, but sometimes one of them would produce surprisingly long legs from under his coat of bristles and rush off to a fresh feeding place. Badgers were busy collecting new bedding, pulling armfuls of bracken along backwards and down into their setts.

Migrant birds were preparing to fly south. The residents were enjoying the harvest of seeds.

It was exactly a year since the female owl had arrived here. Then she had been inexperienced and alone. Now she had produced a family. A fine male bird shared her territory. She had learned to be an expert hunter.

Spreading her soft wings, she flew silently into the friendly night.

Distribution of the Barn Owl

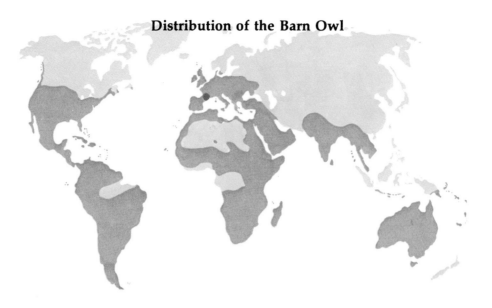

The brown area shows the world distribution.
The red spot marks the location for the story.

A Field Guide to the Territory of the Barn Owl

Below are described the various species which appear throughout this book. See if you can find them all. This will help you to become a better observer of wildlife.

Dormouse *p2*

Dormouse *Muscardinus avellanarius* A very active climber, the dormouse can move quickly and leap between the branches. It passes the winter asleep in a nest of moss in a hollow tree or underground.

Wren *Troglodytes troglodytes* Widespread in Europe and North America, the wren creeps through the undergrowth searching for insects. Its nest is domed with an entrance at one side and often well hidden in a natural cavity.

Wren *p2*

Honeysuckle *p2*

Honeysuckle *Lonicera periclymenum* The beautiful, sweet-scented flowers of this climbing plant attract insects, especially large moths, which feed on their nectar. They carry the pollen from bloom to bloom, ensuring a good crop of berries.

Wood mouse *Sylvaenus sylvaticus* Large eyes and ears show that wood mice are active out of cover where they must be constantly alert. Feeding mostly at night, they eat a wide variety of foods.

Wood mouse *p3*

Hare p5

Hare *Lepus capensis* With its extremely long back legs, the hare can run great distances and escapes enemies by a combination of speed and endurance. It rests in an open 'form' made amongst rank grasses.

Short-tailed vole p4

Short-tailed vole *Microtus agrestis* Short-tailed voles make runway systems through long grass and this gives them cover to move about unseen, but many are eaten by predatory birds and mammals.

Quail p5

Quail *Coturnix coturnix* The quail visits Europe only in summer when it lives in grass or cornfields, preferring to run rather than fly. The male's call sounds like 'wet my lips', repeated several times.

Serin p5

Serin *Serinus serinus* A small finch with a simple, tinkling song that it repeats over and over again. The serin is common around woods and in the gardens and orchards of central and southern Europe.

Cirl Bunting p7

Cirl Bunting *Emberiza cirulus* Living in southern and western Europe, the cirl bunting likes areas with scattered trees or large hedges, but it feeds mainly on the ground, eating seeds and small insects.

House sparrow p7

House sparrow *Passer domesticus* Sparrows seem to like living close to people. Their nests are usually made in holes in buildings, and they feed in towns and villages as often as they do in the fields.

Lapwing p6

Lapwing *Vanellus vanellus* Feeding on insects and snails which they pick from the ground's surface, lapwings live in open fields with short vegetation or bare ground. The eggs and chicks are well camouflaged.

Black-headed gull p6

Black-headed gull *Larus ridibundus* In winter, this gull loses its chocolate-coloured head and has only a dark 'ear patch'. Black-headed gulls often feed on farm land, competing with lapwings for soil invertebrates.

Turtle dove *p9*

Turtle dove *Streptopelia turtur* The purring call of the turtle dove is one of the nicest sounds of summer. A migrant from Africa, it nests in low trees and scrub, and often occurs in large flocks in autumn.

Rabbit *p8*

Rabbit *Oryctolagus cuniculus* Many animals hunt them, but rabbits have sharp eyes and keen ears, and are able to run fast over a short distance, which is usually enough to take them to safety.

Weasel *p8*

Weasel *Mustela nivalis* Small and lithe, the weasel is a tireless hunter, forever popping in and out of holes and crannies as it looks for mice and voles. The larger stoat feeds more on rabbits.

Long-tailed tit *p9*

Long-tailed tit *Aegithelos caudatus* Long-tailed tits build domed nests of feathers and lichens held together with cobwebs and able to stretch as the brood of up to nine youngsters grows larger.

Hen harrier *p8*

Hen harrier *Circus cyaneus* Widespread in Europe, Asia and America, the hen harrier hunts over open country, flying low and slowly to scan the ground, listening carefully for hidden prey.

Swift *p11*

Swift *Apus apus* Swifts are extremely skilled, high-speed fliers which only settle to nest and feed their young. At dusk, the birds fly up high in the sky and spend the night on the wing.

Red-backed shrike *p11*

Red-backed shrike *Lanius collurio* Shrikes have hooked beaks. They are hunters, pouncing on large insects, small mammals and lizards. Sometimes they will impale surplus food on thorns until it is needed.

Long-eared bat *Plecotus auritus* With ears nearly as long as its whole body, the long-eared bat feeds on moths, beetles and other insects which it plucks from the branches and leaves of trees.

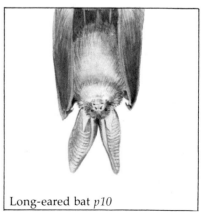

Long-eared bat *p10*

Brown rat *p12*

Brown rat *Rattus norvegicus* Rats are clever and successful animals which live in many habitats. They are wary of strange situations, but soon learn what places are safe to enter and what is safe to eat.

Wild boar *Sus scrofa* Wild pigs live in deciduous woodland, but will come out at night to feed on farmland. They use their strong snouts to dig for bulbs, insects, roots and other food.

Wild boar *p14*

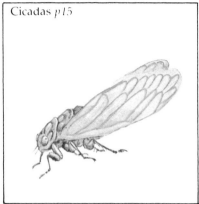
Cicadas *p15*

Cicadas *Cicadidae* Living on plant juices which they suck through a tube-like 'beak', males attract females by clicking a device on the sides of their bodies so rapidly that it sounds like a chirping song.

Nightjar *Caprimulgus caprimulgus* Feeding on insects caught in flight, the nightjar is active only at night. By day, it keeps quite still, relying for concealment on its beautiful, camouflaged plumage.

Nightjar *p14*

Golden oriole *p17*

Golden oriole *Oriolus oriolus* Living in the tree tops, their nests suspended in the forks between high branches, orioles feed on caterpillars and sometimes fruit. They move to Africa in winter.

Wall lizard *Lacerta muralis* Tiny, sharp claws on its feet enable the wall lizard to climb well. Cold-blooded creatures, they are only active when the air is warm and become torpid in cold weather.

Wall lizard *p16*

Fox *p18*

Fox *Vulpes vulpes* Foxes hunt many small creatures from beetles and mice to birds and rabbits. They also eat eggs, fruit, berries and carrion, which means they can live in most areas.

Pyramidal orchid *Anacampetis pyramidalis* These handsome flowers grow mainly on grassland over chalky soils. They have disappeared from many places because the pastures have been ploughed up.

Pyramidal orchid *p18*

Water shrew *p18*

Night heron *p19*

Water shrew *Neomys fodiens* Voracious hunters of beetles and other invertebrates, shrews will die if deprived of food for even a few hours. Water shrews swim and dive well and will also forage over land.

Night heron *Nycticorax nycticorax* Spending the day in cover close to water, night herons fly out at dusk to fish. In Europe, they are rare except in some southern areas.

Hawk moths *p18*

Robin *p20*

Hawk moths *Sphingidae* Hawk moths are strong fliers which feed on flower nectar, sucking it up through the proboscis which is like a double drinking straw that can be curled away neatly when not in use.

Robin *Erithacus rubecula* Birds of woodland, robins will follow animals that turn over the soil – such as rootling pigs – to pick up small insects. This is why they will often come close to gardeners.

Great tit *p20*

Great tit *Parus major* In summer, great tits feed mainly on insects and spiders in the trees. They also forage on the ground, especially in autumn and winter when there are berries and seeds to find.

Red squirrel *Sciurus vulgaris* Squirrels find most of their food in the trees but they also forage on the ground. If they are frightened, they will always make a dash for the nearest tree.

Red squirrel *p20*

Polecat *p21*

Polecat *Mustela putorius* Though related to the weasel, the polecat is more than twice its size and able to take much larger prey. It marks its territory with an unpleasant smelling substance.

Beech *Fagus sylvatica* Beeches flourish on chalk soils and grow widely in Europe. The leaves cast such deep shade that few other plants can grow beneath a beech unless they flower early in spring, before the tree has leaves.

Beech *p20*

Hoopoe p22

Subalpine warbler p23

Hoopoe *Upopa epops* A summer visitor to southern Europe, the hoopoe's name comes from its call, a hollow-sounding 'hoo pooh pooh'. It probes in the soil with its long beak for grubs, worms and insects.

Subalpine warbler *Sylvia cantillans* Like other warblers, this species is an insect eater inhabiting dense scrub cover and favouring sunny hill slopes. On migration, it may be seen in the lowlands.

Hedgehog p24

Pheasant p25

Hedgehog *Erinaceus europaeus* Neither fast nor fierce, hedgehogs are protected by their spiny coats, rolling into a ball when danger threatens. They can swim, and eat insects, slugs, snails and worms.

Pheasant *Phasianus colchicus* Originally found in south-west Asia, pheasants were introduced into Europe long ago. On many estates, young birds are reared so that there are plenty to be shot for sport and eating.

Badger p25

Noctule p25

Badger *Meles meles* Badger families excavate extensive underground tunnel systems and fill their sleeping quarters with dry bedding of grass, leaves and bracken. They are mainly nocturnal.

Noctule *Nyctalus noctula* Noctules are active at dusk and sometimes by day. Like other bats, they pass the winter hibernating in dark places, not emerging until flying insects are again plentiful in spring.

Nightingale p25

Nightingale *Luscinia megarhynchos* A summer visitor to Europe, the nightingale winters in Africa. It prefers light, open woodland with dense undergrowth. Males sing by day as well as at night.

Lombardy poplar *Populus nigra 'italica'* This tree is easy to recognize because the branches grow upwards close to the trunk, making it look very slender. Often, rows of them are planted alongside a road to form an avenue.

Lombardy poplar p24

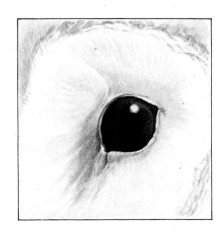

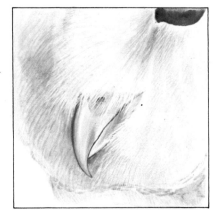

Barn Owl *Tyto alba*

Eye the eyes look forwards, giving the binocular vision needed to judge distance when grasping prey. Very large and light sensitive, they give the owl good vision even on the darkest night.

Beak The hooked tip of the beak is used to pull large prey apart for feeding the chicks. The adults usually swallow small prey whole after crushing its skull with the beak.

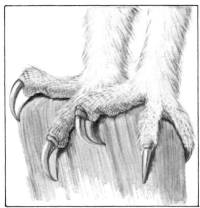

Feet Owls have long legs to reach out after fleeing prey. Their feet have sharp talons, and there are large lumps on the undersides of the toes, which help the owl to grip wriggling prey.

Flight Owls can fly silently because their flight feathers have soft, almost furry fringes. Silent flight enables owls to hear the quiet sounds of prey without being heard.

First published 1981
© 1981 J. M. Dent & Sons Ltd and Legatoria Editoriale Giovanni Olivotto L.E.G.O.S.P.A.
All rights reserved.
This book is set in VIP Palatino
by Trident Graphics Limited, Reigate, Surrey
Printed in Italy by Legatoria Editoriale Giovanni Olivotto L.E.G.O.S.P.A., Vicenza
for J. M. Dent & Sons Limited
Aldine House, Welbeck Street, London

British Library Cataloguing in Publication Data

Riley, Terry
Year of the Barn Owl
1 Barn Owl – Juvenile Literature
2 Birds – Juvenile Literature
I Title   II Andrews, John, b.1939
598.9′7   QL696.S85

ISBN 0–460–06958–6